The Spring of Joy: Poems

Mary Webb

THE SPRING OF JOY: POEMS

By

Mary Webb

1917

CONTENTS

Green rain

Mischief: to a bee

Foxgloves

The water ousel

Starlings

Fairy-led

The secret joy

In April

The happy life

Market day

'You are very brown'

Rose-berries

In dark weather

The garden in winter

Snowdrop time

A rainy day

The spirit of earth

To life

'Like a poppy on a tower'

Prescences

The night sky (1916)

The plain in Autumn

The elf

My own town

The wood

Viroconium

Swallows

Heaven's tower

Dust

The watcher

The little hill

The fallen poplar

The elfin valley

A summer day

'The birds will sing'

The hills of Heaven

Farewell to beauty

Good-bye to morning

Why?

Beyond

Safe

To the world

A farewell

The neighbour's children

An old woman

Going for the milk

To a little girl begging

Anne's book

On receiving a box of spring flowers in London

Freedom

Spring in the west

To a poet in April

To a blackbird singing in London

The little sorrow

Treasures (for G.E.M)

The difference

Winter sunrise

Hunger

The lad out there

To mother (Christmas, 1920)

Alone

Eros

When the thorn blows

'How short a while'

'Be still, you little leaves'

'Ah, do not be so sweet!'

Autumn

November

Humble folk

Winter

The thought

Little things

The shell

A hawthorn berry

The snowdrop

The vision

The vagrant

The wild rose

Thresholds

The door

The land within

The ancient gods

Colomen

Green rain

Into the scented woods we'll go
And see the blackthorn swim in snow.
High above, in the budding leaves,
A brooding dove awakes and grieves;
The glades with mingled music stir,
And wildly laughs the woodpecker.
When blackthorn petals pearl the breeze,
There are the twisted hawthorn trees
Thick-set with buds, as clear and pale
As golden water or green hail—
As if a storm of rain had stood
Enchanted in the thorny wood,
And, hearing fairy voices call,
Hung poised, forgetting how to fall.

Mischief to a bee

O Bee!
While I believed you gathering in the sun
Nectar so busily,
What have you done?

My violet,
More white than well-bleached linen, you have kissed:
Her white she must forget
In amethyst.

See, see,
How you have meddled with the snowy clover,
Making her ivory
Blush like a lover!

My primroses,
That gave a greenish, pale moonshine,
O mischief-making bees!
Are red as wine.

Foxgloves

The foxglove bells, with lolling tongue,
Will not reveal what peals were rung
In Faery, in Faery,
A thousand ages gone.
All the golden clappers hang
As if but now the changes rang;
Only from the mottled throat
Never any echoes float.
Quite forgotten, in the wood,
Pale, crowded steeples rise;
All the time that they have stood
None has heard their melodies.
Deep, deep in wizardry
All the foxglove belfries stand.
Should they startle over the land,
None would know what bells they be.
Never any wind can ring them,
Nor the great black bees that swing them —
Every crimson bell, down-slanted,
Is so utterly enchanted.

The water ousel

Where on the wrinkled stream the willows lean,
And fling a very ecstasy of green
Down the dim crystal, and the chestnut tree
Admires her large-leaved shadow, swift and free
A water ousel came, with such a flight
As archangels might envy. Soft and bright,
Upon a water-kissing bough she lit
And washed and preened her silver breast, though it
Was dazzling fair before. Then twittering
She sang, and made obeisance to the Spring.
And in the wavering amber at her feet
Her silent shadow, with obedience meet,
Made her quick, imitative curtsies too.
Maybe she dreamed a nest, so safe, so dear,
Where the keen spray leaps whitely to the weir;
And smooth, warm eggs that hold a mystery;
And stirrings of life, and twitterings that she
Is passionately glad of; and a breast
As silver white as hers, which without rest
Or languor, borne by spread wings swift and strong,
Shall fly upon her service all day long.
She hears a presage in the ancient thunder
Of the silken fall, and her small soul in wonder
Makes preparation as she deems most right,
Re-purifying what before was white
Against the day when, like a beautiful dream,
Two little ousels shall fly with her down-stream,
And even the poor, dumb shadow-bird shall flit
With two small shadows following after it.

Starlings

When the blue summer night
Is short and safe and light,
How should the starlings any more remember
The fearful, trembling times of dark December?
They mimic in their glee,
With impudent jocosity,
The terrible ululation of the owls
That prey
On just such folk as they.
'Tu-whoo!' And rusty-feathered fledglings, pressed
Close in the nest
Amid the chimney-stacks, are good all day
If their indulgent father will but play
At owls,
With predatory howls
And hoots and shrieks and whistlings wild and dread.
Says one small bird,
With lids drawn up, cosily tucked in bed,
'Such things were never heard
By me or you.
They are not true.'

Fairy-led

The fairy people flouted me,
Mocked me, shouted me—
They chased me down the dreamy hill and beat me with a wand.
Within the wood they found me, put spells on me and bound me
And left me at the edge of day in John the miller's pond.

Beneath the eerie starlight
Their hair shone curd-white;
Their bodies were all twisted like a lichened apple-tree;
Feather-light and swift they moved,
And never one the other loved,
For all were full of ancient dreams and dark designs on me.

With noise of leafy singing
And white wands swinging,
They marched away amid the grass that swayed to let them through.
Between the yellow tansies
Their eyes, like purple pansies,
Peered back on me before they passed all trackless in the dew.

The secret of joy

Face to face with the sunflower,
Cheek to cheek with the rose,
We follow a secret highway
Hardly a traveller knows.
The gold that lies in the folded bloom
We eat of the heart of the forest
With innocent stealth.
We know the ancient roads
In the leaf of a nettle,
And bathe in the blue profound
Of a speedwell petal.

In April

In April, in April
My heart is set
Where the pansy and the violet
And the daffodil,
And close-folded lilies grow
In borders dark with melted snow.
Wakening there from wintry sleep
With every bud I sunward creep.
The empurpled crocuses, that dare
With delicate veins the dawn-cold air,
Cradle me in their chalices
Amid the golden sediment.
There I lie in warm content
And listen to the velvet bees,
Watching their dark blue shadows fall
Along the half-transparent wall.
When the sharp-pointed grasses prick
Upward, all passionate to be free,
I share their conflict, fierce and quick,
With the earthen will; I know their glee.
In the star-tinted pimpernel
I hear the silver tongue of rain;
And learn the perfume thrushes smell,
Which makes their song as keen as pain;
And see, where long-lashed daisies crowd,
New revelations in the cloud.
That is why, when old I grow
And near my end, I shall not know.
For every year my heart is set
With the pansy and the violet
And the daffodil:
Submerged within their beauty, I
Transcend my poor mortality.

The happy life

No silks have I, no furs nor feathers,
But one old gown that knows all weathers;
No veils nor parasols nor lace,
But rough hands and a tanned face.
Yet the soft, crinkled leaves are mine
Where pale, mysterious veins shine,
And laced larches upon the blue,
And grey veils where the moon looks through;
The cries of birds across the lawns
In dark and teeming April dawns;
The sound of wings at the door-sill,
Where grows the wet-eyed tormentil;
The ripe berry's witcheries-
Its perfect round that satisfies;
And the gay scent of the wood I burn,
And the slap of butter in a busy churn.

Market day

Who'll walk the fields with us to town,
In an old coat and a faded gown?
We take our roots and country sweets
Where high walls shade the steep old streets,
And golden bells and silver chimes
Ring up and down the sleepy times.
The morning mountains smoke like fires;
The sun spreads out his shining wires;
The mower in the half-mown leasur
Sips his tea and takes his pleasure.
Along the lanes slow waggons amble;
The sad-eyed calves awake and gamble;
The foal that lay so sorrowful
Is playing in the grasses cool.
By slanting ways, in slanting sun,
Through startled lapwings now we run
Along the pale green hazel-path,
Through April's lingering aftermath
Of lady's smock and lady's slipper;
We stay to watch a nesting dipper.
The rabbits eye us while we pass,
Out of the sorrel-crimson grass;
The blackbird sings, without a fear,
Where honeysuckle horns blow clear—
Cool ivory stained with true vermilion;
And here, within a silk pavilion,
Small caterpillars lie at ease.
The endless shadows of the trees
Are painted purple and cobalt;
Grandiloquent, the rook-files halt,
Each one aware of you and me,
And full of conscious dignity.
Our shoes are golden as we pass
With pollen from the pansied grass.
Beneath an elder—set anew

With large clean plates to catch the dew —
On fine white cheese and bread we dine:
The clear brook-water tastes like wine.
If all folk lived with labour sweet
Of their own busy hands and feet,
Such marketing, it seems to me,
Would make an end of poverty.

'You are very brown'

Elves of the hollow and the dewpond still,
Take pity! Gather for me dew as chill
As ice, and glittering-pure as early dawn,
From pink-tipped daisies on the printless lawn
And the transparent cups of apple-bloom,
And lily bells, to save me from this doom
Of being so brown!
Bring me an unguent made of scented roots;
Pomander of green herbs and scarlet fruits,
Verbena leaves, mallow and melilot,
And balmy rosemary, that I may not
Be brown!
O sweet wild rose,
You have so fair a colour in your face!
Spare me a blush; take from me this disgrace
Of being so brown!
Lilies, you do not guess,
In your pale loveliness,
The grief it is to hear,
In a voice dispassionate and clear,
'You're very brown!'

Rose-berries

The green pine-needles shiver glassily,
Each cased in ice. Harsh winter, grey and dun,
Shuts out the sun.
But with live, scarlet fire,
Enfolding seed of sweet Junes yet to be,
Rose-berries melt the snow, and burn above
The thorny briar,
Like beauty with its deathless seed of love.

In dark weather

Against the gaunt, brown-purple hill
The bright brown oak is wide and bare;
A pale-brown flock is feeding there—
Contented, still.

No bracken lights the bleak hill-side;
No leaves are on the branches wide;
No lambs across the fields have cried;
—Not yet.

But whorl by whorl the green fronds climb;
The ewes are patient till their time;
The warm buds swell beneath the rime—
For life does not forget.

The garden in winter

The winter sun that rises near the south
Looks coldly on my garden of cold clay;
Like some old dotard with a bitter mouth,
Shrugs his grey robe to his ears and creeps away.
Come down the mountains, April! with young eyes,
And roguish daisy-children trooping after,
Draw from the sullen clay red peonies,
Bring back the sun as a stripling full of laughter!

Snowdrop time

Ah, hush! Tread softly through the rime,
For there will be a blackbird singing, or a thrush.
Like coloured beads the elm-buds flush:
All the trees dream of leaves and flowers and light.
And see! The northern bank is much more white
Than frosty grass, for now is snowdrop time.

A rainy day

With weights of tears the bluebell broke,
The tall white campion wept in sleeping,
And all the humming honey-folk
A fast were keeping.

The spririt of the earth

Love me—and I will give into your hands
The rare, enamelled jewels of my lands,
Flowers red and blue,
Tender with air and dew.

From far green armouries of pools and meres
I'll reach for you my lucent sheaves of spears—
The singing falls,
Where the lone ousel calls.

When, like a passing light upon the sea,
Your wood-bird soul shall clap her wings and flee,
She shall but nest
More closely in my breast.

To life

Fair, fierce Life! What will you do with me?
What will you make me?
Take me and break me,
Hurt me, or love me,
But throne me not lonely and safely above thee,
Sweet Life!

Radiant, terrible Life! See now, I offer thee
Body and spirit.
Let me inherit
Agony—wonder:
But leave me not icily, numbly asunder,
Dear Life!

Like a poppy on a tower

Like a poppy on a tower
The present hour!
The wind stirs, the wind awakes,
Beneath its feet the tower shakes.
All down the crannied wall
Torn scarlet petals fall,
Like scattered fire or shivered glass
And drifting with their motion pass
Torn petals of blue shadow
From the grey tower to the green meadow.

Prescences

There is a presence on the lonely hill,
Lovely and chill:
There is an emanation in the wood,
Half understood.
They come upon me like an evening cloud,
Stranger than moon-rise, whiter than a shroud.
I shall not see them plain
Ever again,
Though in my childhood days
I knew their ways.
They are as secret as the black cloud-shadows
Sliding along the ripe midsummer grass;
With a breath-taking majesty they pass,
Down by the water in the mournful meadows;
Out of the pale pink distance at the falling
Of dusk they gaze—remote, summoning, chill;
Sweetly in April I have heard them calling
Where through black ash-buds gleams the purple hill.

The night sky (1916)

The moon, beyond her violet bars,
From towering heights of thunder-cloud,
Sheds calm upon our scarlet wars,
To soothe a world so small, so loud.
And little clouds like feathered spray,
Like rounded waves on summer seas,
Or frosted panes on a winter day,
Float in the dark blue silences.
Within their foam, transparent, white,
Like flashing fish the stars go by
Without a sound across the night.
In quietude and secrecy
The white, soft lightnings feel their way
To the boundless dark and back again,
With less stir than a gnat makes
In its little joy, its little pain.

The plain in Autumn

A solemn land of long-fulfilled desires
Is this, and year by year the self-same fires
Burn in the trees. The untarnished colours keep
The sweetness of the young earth's infant sleep:
Beyond the plain, beneath the evening star,
The burnished hills like stately peacocks are.
Great storms march out. The flocks across the grass
Make their low plaint while the swift shadows pass:
Memoried deep in Hybla, the wild bee
Sings in the purple-fruited damson tree:
And, darkly sweet as Ruth, the dairy-maid
By the lean, laughing shepherd is waylaid.

The elf

A fair town is Shrewsbury—
The world over
You'll hardly find a fairer,
In its fields of clover
And rest-harrow, ringed
By hills where curlews call,
And, drunken from the heather,
Black bees fall.
Poplars, by Severn,
Lean hand in hand,
Like golden girls dancing
In elfland.

Early there come travelling
On market day
Old men and young men
From far away,
With red fruits of the orchard
And dark fruits of the hill,
Dew-fresh garden stuff
And mushrooms chill,
Honey from the brown skep,
Brown eggs, and posies
Of gillyflowers and Lent lilies
And blush roses.

And sometimes, in a branch of blossom,
Or a lily deep,
An elf comes, plucked with the flower
In her sleep;
Lifts a languid wing, slow and weary,
Veined like a shell;
Listens, with eyes dark and eerie,
To the church bell;
Creeps further within her shelter

Of lilac or lily,
Weaving enchantments,
Laughing stilly.

Neither bells in the steeple
Nor books, old and brown,
Can disenchant the people
In the slumbering town.

My own town

In this old town I know so well
I have dwelt in heaven and in hell,
And seen its folk go to and fro
With faces of unthinkable woe,
Ferocious as primaeval beasts,
Or rapt as angels at their feasts,
When close they press in silver rows
While up and down the chalice goes,
Made of a sapphire, filled to the brim
With God. I have seen them walk like kings
Pondering on majestic things.
And where the gossip gables lean
Chatting, I've met with faces mean
With meanness past all grace or cure.
As long as those blue hills endure,
That stand around the gracious plain
Which circles-in the town, and rain
Marches across the corn, and tears
Weigh down the harvest of our years,
So long what I have seen and felt,
When in its churches I have knelt
And wandered by the evening stream
And seen the April roadways gleam,
Shall live. And when the traffic's hum
Is gone, the busy market dumb
As a winter bee, and all the spires
Are melted in the hungry fires
Of Time, and not a house remains—
Then here, upon the empty plains,
Encircled by the changeless heights,
As changeless through the days and nights
As they, in colours that cannot fade,
Shall stand the town that I have made
With golden house and silver steeple
And a strange uplifted people,

Who in their charmed streets shall go
Hushed with a tremendous woe
And a joy as deep and vast
As shadows that the mountains cast.
And I shall dwell where once unknown
I passed, and all shall be my own,
Because I built of joy and tears
A city that defies the years.

The wood

Tall, feathered birches, on the tides of air,
Wash to and fro, like seaweeds fine and fair,
And deep in leaf and blossom from all eyes
The rope-walk of the honeysuckle lies.
There, crimson foxgloves taper slenderly,
And the brown-seeded brake grows ten feet high.
There are strange, flaming toad-stools, and the berries.
Of ash and rose, that shine like scarlet cherries.
The rose-bay willowherb, in her bridal hour,
Blooms, and the larch sets forth her rosy flower.
Kestrels are there, and tawny foxes play
Amid the shadows in the early day.
Low cry the sheep, and leave their shining fleece
On the long vines of purple blackberries.
High in their minstrel gallery above,
Hidden in fretted leaves, dove answers dove,
And like a distant bell, melodiously
Haunting these glades, the music of the bee
Chimes all the summer. . . . Like a bird, with wings
Dusky and silent, I would flit through spring's
Wistful, immaculate colours; through the dream
And hush of summer; down the rush and gleam
Of autumn; and when winter, with a moan,
Swept through the freezing wood aloof, alone,
Prisoning the pine needles in shining, hollow
Cases of ice, yet the brown bird would follow.
Light as a last year's leaf I'd flutter by,
With the sad note of finches in July.
Still should the foxgloves gather, spring by spring;
Still should the feathered birches wash and swing
Upon the tides of air, and in the sun
Each autumn should the little foxes run,
While I in shadow dwelt. Dark on the sky
Should kestrels anchor, watching warily

For small brown birds: but in the meadow green
I'd fearless flit, beneath their gaze unseen.

Viroconium

Virocon—Virocon—
Still the ancient name rings on
And brings, in the untrampled wheat,
The tumult of a thousand feet.

Where trumpets rang and men marched by,
None passes but the dragon-fly.
Athwart the grassy town, forlorn,
The lone dor-beetle blows his horn,

The poppy standards droop and fall
Above one rent and mournful wall:
In every sunset-flame it burns,
Yet towers unscathed when day returns.

And still the breaking seas of grain
Flow havenless across the plain:
The years wash on, their spindrift leaps
Where the old city, dreaming, sleeps.

Grief lingers here, like mists that lie
Across the dawns of ripe July;
On capital and corridor
The pathos of the conqueror.

The pillars stand, with alien grace,
In churches of a younger race;
The chiselled column, black and rough,
Becomes a roadside cattle-trough:

The skulls of men who, right or wrong,
Still wore the splendour of the strong,
Are shepherds' lanterns now, and shield
Their candles in the lambing field.

But when, through evening's open door,
Two lovers tread the broken floor,
And the wild-apple petals fall
Round passion's scarlet festival;

When cuckoos call from the green gloom
Where dark, shelving forests loom;
When foxes bark beside the gate,
And the grey badger seeks his mate

There haunts within them secretly
One that lives while empires die,
A shrineless god whose songs abide
Forever in the countryside.

Swallows

The swallows pass in restless companies.
Against the pink-flowered may, one shining breast
Throbs momentary music—then, possessed
With motion, sweeps on some new enterprise.
Unquiet in heart, I hear their eager cries
And see them dart to their nests beneath the eaves;
Within my spirit is a voice that grieves,
Reminding me of empty autumn skies.
Nor can we rest in Nature's dear delight:
June droops to winter, and the sun droops west.
Flight is our life. We build our crumbling nest
Beneath the dark eaves of the infinite,
We sing our song in beauty's fading tree,
And flash forth, migrant, into mystery.

Heaven's tower

Hark! The wind in heaven's tower
Moaneth for the passing hour.

Heaven's tower is broad and high;
In its quiet chambers lie
Laughing lovers. Rose and apple
Are their cheeks. Pale shadows dapple
All the floors, by night and day,
From sun-ray and moon-ray
Shining through the hearted leaves
Of the dark tree that lips the eaves.
Where the topmost turret ends,
Grey as the parting word of friends,
Sadly sways a silver bell,
And evermore it tolls farewell.
In all weathers, feathered brown
As doves, moaning, up and down,
Hover the disconsolate
Souls that never found a mate.
But within, so safe, so deep
Lapt in joy, the lovers sleep,
Pillowed cool in violets, pansies,
Delicate hopes and tender fancies.
How should they, so closely lying,
With clasping limbs, hear the crying
Of the wind from north or south?
While they murmur, mouth on mouth,
The grievous bell they do not hear,
Every toll a silver tear;
Nor dream they that the mystic, tall
Tree whose leaves like shadows fall
And fill the tower with whispering breath,
Bears the purple fruit of death.

Dust

On burning ploughlands, faintly blue with wheat,
A three-horse roller toils, the wandering dust
A nimbus round it. Shadow-coloured hills
Huddle beyond—hump-shouldered, kingly-headed
Or eel-shaped; sinister, tortured—waiting still,
Beneath the purposeful, secretive sky,
The multitudinous years
That soon or late will melt them.
So I have felt them
In all their static beauty only fit for tears,
Like those that toil along the blood-red weald
With their own death-dust round them for sole glory
Under the falcon wings
Of dawn, the red night's carrion-swoop,
The intolerable emptiness of air.

Long, long ago I thought on all these things:
Long, long ago I loved them.

The watcher

Where the black woods grow sparse and die,
A giant broods against the sky.
The storm his chlamys, and his head
Bent to the spirits of the dead.

The windhover, floating like a leaf,
Passes him safely, clear of grief.
The auburn doves within the wood
Have pondered him and understood.

The wandering breaths of cattle come
Towards his fastness, and the hum
From paper homes of wasps, and cries
Of bees in their refectories.

The evening smoke ascends again
Out of the sapphire-circled plain,
And to the oatfield, pale as wax,
A black swift hurtles like an axe.

There shadow, with her gentle fingers,
Soothes all the dappled land; she lingers
On little croft and ample field,
With their benign and wistful yield.

The Watcher on the summit stands
With a blue goblet in his hands;
He slowly drinks the glimmering years,
The sparkling laughter and the tears.

He is not angered nor forgiving;
He does not sever dead from living,
But sees them all as long gone by,
Returning in futurity.

And still he counts, with stooping head,
The spirits of the living dead—
A soul or two in every field,
And in the furrowed, crimson weald;

And some in every orchard-close,
Who pruned the cherry and the rose,
And waited for the damson sweet,
And plodded through the brittle wheat.

The little hill

This is the hill, ringed by the misty shire—
The mossy, southern hill,
The little hill where larches climb so high.
Among the stars aslant
They chant;
Along the purple lower slopes they lie
In lazy golden smoke, more faint, more still
Than the pale woodsmoke of the cottage fire.
Here some calm Presence takes me by the hand
And all my heart is lifted by the chant
Of them that lean aslant
In golden smoke, and sing, and softly bend:
And out from every larch-bole steals a friend.

The fallen polar

Never any more shall the golden sun
Make of your leaves, my dainty one,
Ardent shields of silver-green,
With cool blue sky set in between.

Never any more in the chilly night
Your boughs shall move on the sad starlight,
Softly unbound by the eager air,
As a lover unbinds his lady's hair.

Never any more, O poplar tree!
Shall dawn awaken your song for me;
For a wind came down from the granite bill,
And you, the friend of my heart, lie still.

The elfin valley

By this low rock pool, dark and sweet,
Where panting Summer cools her feet,
No creature stirs, except the leaves
That sometimes glide along the air
Like children down a shallow stair,
And nothing strives or grieves.

The lone ferns drip from every frond.
Green, round and polished lies the pond,
A mirror for the stooping moon.
Above, the fall is straight and white,
A comet in a sultry night,
Among the leaves of June.

All spell-bound in the drowsy gloom,
Grey-leaved, white-flowered, the mulleins bloom;
And if a swallow suddenly
Should cut the pool with one sharp wing,
Or if a thrush come here to sing,
It seems a prodigy.

A lone green valley, good for sheep,
Where still the ancient fairies keep
Their right of way and copyhold
All night with mullein torches. Far
Within the stream, a dreaming star
Has laid a spell of gold.

A summer day

Long aisles of larches stretch away,
Mysterious, dim;
And in their branches breezes play
A solemn hymn.

Across the glades the larches fling
Their shadows, stirred
Faintly, but no bird lifts a wing,
And sings no bird.

The flecks of sunlight shift and crowd
So goldenly,
And softly faints the last thin cloud
From the blue sky.

'The birds will sing'

The birds will sing when I am gone
To stranger-folk with stranger-ways.
Without a break they'll whistle on
In close and flowery orchard deeps,
Where once I loved them, nights and days,
And never reck of one that weeps.

The bud that slept within the bark
When I was there, will break her bars—
A small green flame from out the dark—
And round into a world, and spread
Beneath the silver dews and stars,
Nor miss my bent, attentive head.

The hills of heaven

We were in the hills of heaven
But yesterday!
All was so changeless, quiet, fair,
All swam so deep in golden air;
White-tapered chestnuts, seven by seven,
Went down the shady valleys there
Where daffodils are, and linnets play;
And singing streams of yellow and brown
Through golden mimulus ran down.
Ah, haunted were the hills of heaven,
Where no tree falls and none is riven,
Where the frail valley-lilies stay
Becalmed in beauty, every leaf
And every flower! Ah, bitter grief—
Remembering the hills of heaven
And yesterday!

Farewell to beauty

'Their being is to be perceived.'
- BERKELEY

Let fall your golden showers, laburnum tree!
Break the grey casket of your buds for me—
Soon I shall go where never gold is seen,
And who will be with you as I have been?

Quick with your silver notes, O silver bird!
Wistful, I listen for the song I heard
Many a day, but soon shall hear no more,
For summoning winds are out along the shore.

All things so early fade—swiftly pass over,
As autumn bees desert the withering clover.
Now, with the bee, I sing immortal June;
How soon both song and bee are gone—how soon!

Who'll watch the clover secretly unclose?
Finger the sycamore buds, afire with rose?
Trace the mauve veins of the anemone?
Know the peculiar scent of every tree?

Maybe the solemn hill, the enchanted plain
'Will be but arable and wild again,
Losing the purple bloom they wore for me—
The dreaming god I could so clearly see.

Good-bye to morning

I will say good-bye to morning, with her eyes
Of gold, her shell-pale robe and crocus-crown.
Once her green veils enmeshed me, following down
The dewy hills of heaven: with young surprise
The daisies eyed me, and the pointed leaves
Came swiftly in green fire to meet the sun:
The elves from every hollow, one by one,
Laughed shrilly. But the wind of evening grieves
In the changing wood. Like people sad and old,
The white-lashed daisies sleep, and on my sight
Looms my new sombre comrade, ancient night.
His eyes dream dark on death; all stark and cold
His fingers, and on his wild forehead gleams
My morning wreath of withered and frozen dreams.

Why?

Why did you come, with your enkindled eyes
And mountain-look, across my lower way,
And take the vague dishonour from my day
By luring me from paltry things, to rise
And stand beside you, waiting wistfully
The looming of a larger destiny?

Why did you with strong fingers fling aside
The gates of possibility, and say
With vital voice the words I dream to-day?
Before, I was not much unsatisfied:
But since a god has touched me and departed,
I run through every temple, broken-hearted.

Beyond

Far beyond, far beyond,
Deeper than the glassy pond,
My shivering spirit sits and weeps
And never sleeps.

Like the autumn dove that grieves,
Darkly hid in dove-like leaves,
So I moan within a woe
None may know.

Safe

Under a blossoming tree
Let me lie down,
With one blackbird to sing to me
In the evenings brown.
Safe from the world's long importunity—
The endless talk, the critical, sly stare,
The trifling social days—and unaware
Of all the bitter thoughts they have of me,
Low in the grass, deep in the daisies,
I shall sleep sound, safe from their blames and praises.

To the world

You took the rare blue from my cloudy sky;
You shot the one bird in my silent wood;
You crushed my rose—one rose alone had I.
You have not known. You have not understood.

I would have shown you pictures I have seen
Of unimagined mountains, plains and seas;
I would have made you songs of leafy green,
If you had left me some small ecstasies.

Now let the one dear field be only field,
That was a garden for the mighty gods.
Take you its corn. I keep its better yield—
The glory that I found within its clods.

A farewell

Beloved, once more I take the winter way
Through solitude's dark mountains, purple and cold
As frozen pansies, toward my house of clay
Where winds shall drink my tears, and shadows fold.

I dare not dwell so near to ecstasy
Lest I grow reckless, seeing the dear, the good,
And so, beseeching for it childishly,
Should spoil its beauty and my womanhood.

Yet will the breathless moments when you smiled,
Looking upon me, haunt me. It is not well
Remembering, when winter floods are wild,
Becalmed lilies and the summer's spell.

Farewell, beloved! Since you have grown too dear,
I must be gone. I take my pilgrimage
In haste—so much I love you, so much fear.
Wisdom may grow from tears, peace fall with age.

The neighbour's children

They run to meet me, clinging to my dress,
The neighbour's children. With a wild unrest
And sobbings of a strange, fierce tenderness,
I snatch them to my breast.
But *my* baby, ah! *my* baby
Weepeth—weepeth
In the far loneliness of nonentity,
And holds his little spirit hands to me,
Crying 'Mother!' and nearer creepeth;
Beats on my heart's lit window anxiously,
Shivering and sobbing, 'Mother, let me in!
Give me my rosy dress, my delicate dress
Of apple-blossom flesh, dark eyes like flowers,
And warm mouth kissed by a red anemone.
Give me my toys—the hills, the seas, the sun,
Loud song, wild winds, the morning's cloudy towers.
Give hands to hold and ears to hear and feet to run.
Give me my lesson books—fear, love and sin—
All hell to brave, all heaven to win!'

Then, shadowy, wild and wan,
A little face peers in,
Except in dreams unknown even to me,
And like a summer cloud is gone.
It is the neighbour's children, playing near,
With voices ringing clear.
But far in twilight, like a moon-awakened bird,
Was that another, fainter laugh I heard?

An old woman

They bring her flowers—red roses heavily sweet,
White pinks and Mary-lilies and a haze
Of fresh green ferns; around her head and feet
They heap more flowers than she in all her days
Possessed. She sighed once—'Posies aren't for me;
They cost too much.'
Yet now she sleeps in them, and cannot see
Or smell or touch.

Now in a new and ample gown she lies—
White as a daisy-bud, as soft and warm
As those she often saw with longing eyes,
Passing some bright shop window in a storm.
Then, when her flesh could feel, how harsh her wear!
Not warm nor white.
This would have pleased her once. She does not care
At all to-night.

They give her tears—affection's frailest flowers—
And fold her close in praise and tenderness:
She does not heed. Yet in those empty hours
If there had come, to cheer her loneliness,
But one red rose in youth's rose-loving day,
A smile, a tear,
It had been good. But now she goes her way
And does not hear.

Going for the milk

Going for the milk—
A toddling child with skin like curds,
On a May morning in a charm of birds:

Going for the milk
With laughing, teasing lads, at seventeen,
With rosy cheeks and breast as soft as silk—
Eh! what a mort of years between!

Going for the milk
Through my Jim's garden, past the bush o' balm,
With my first baby sleeping on my arm:

It's fifty year, come Easter, since that day;
The work'us ward is cold, my eyes be dim;
Never no more I'll go the flowery way,
Fetching the milk. I drink the pauper's skim,
And mind me of those summer days, and Jim
Telling me as my breast was soft as silk—
And that first day I missed to fetch the milk.

To a little girl begging

Poor little traveller, lost in night!
God made a miracle, I know,
To give you life—tears and delight,
And ecstasy and ancient woe.
Yet barefoot in the snow you stand,
Beseeching bread with shaking hand.

Poor baby, with your wistful face!
When you are grown a man, and tall,
You'll have the kingly, simple grace,
The smile that makes a festival.
Yet from the dark your hungry eyes
Behold the cook-shop's paradise.

Anne's book

And so, Anne Everard, in those leafy Junes
Long withered; in those ancient, dark Decembers,
Deep in the drift of time, haunted by tunes
Long silent; you, beside the homely embers,
Or in some garden fragrant and precise
Were diligent and attentive all day long!
Fashioning with bright wool and stitches nice
Your sampler, did you hear the thrushes' song
Wistfully? While, in orderly array,
Six rounded trees grew up; the alphabet,
Stout and uncompromising, done in grey;
The Lord's Prayer, and your age, in violet;
Did you, Anne Everard, dream from hour to hour
How the young wind was crying on the bill,
And the young world was breaking into flower?
With small head meekly bent, all mute and still,
Earnest to win the promised great reward,
Did you not see the birds, at shadow-time,
Come hopping all across the dewy sward?
Did you not hear the bells of Faery chime
Liquidly, where the brittle hyacinths grew?
Your dream—attention; diligence, your aim!
And when the last long needleful was through,
When, laboured for so long, the guerdon came—
Thomson, his *Seasons*, neatly bound in green—
How brightly would the golden letters shine!
Ah! many a petalled May the moon has seen
Since Anne—attentive, diligent, *aetat* nine—
Puckering her young brow, read the stately phrases.
Sampler and book are here without a stain—
Only Anne Everard lies beneath the daisies;
Only Anne Everard will not come again.

On receiving a bow of spring flower in London

So the old, dear freemasonry goes on—
The busy life, the laughter-under-sod,
The leafy hosts with spear and gonfalon
Guarding the earthy mysteries of God.

I did not think the violets came so soon,
Yet here are five, and all my room is sweet;
And here's an aconite—a golden moon
Shining where all her raying leaflets meet;

And here a snowdrop, finely veined—ah, see!
Fresh from the artist's hand, and folded close:
She only waits the sunshine and the bee;
Then she will open like a golden rose.

Freedom

When on the moss-green hill the wandering wind
Drowses, and lays his brazen trumpet down,
When snow-fed waters gurgle, cold and brown,
And wintered birds creep from the stacks to find
Solace, while each bright eye begins to see
A visionary nest in every tree—
Let us away, out of the murky day
Of sullen towns, into the silver noise
Of woods where every bud has found her way
Sunward, and every leaf has found a voice.

Spring in the west

Soon amid the inviolable places
Will green, rustling steeples chime again
With the sweet, glassy bell-notes of the wren.
Soon the plain shall lie beneath blue spaces—
Bold and broad and ruddy in the sun,
Long and lean to the moon when day is done.

Soon will come the strange, heart-lifting season
When through the dark, still dawns, where nothing was,
Steals the mysterious whisper of growing grass;
And a joy like pain possesses the soul, without reason,
Between the budding of day and the lapse of night,
With the clear, cold scent of wet starlight.

To a poet in April

The world has praised your leafy songs,
And you, in singing them, have made
Rich folk forget their gains and wrongs
And poor folk love the hawthorn shade.
While year by year your fame has grown,
You had one silent friend unknown.

And on those gleamy April days
That hurt my soul with too much bliss
When I am wandering woodland ways,
A-bloom with twining ecstasies,
You speak my joy in silver words
I thought none knew so well, but birds.

So deep within a blossomy cave
With musing blackbirds in the trees,
While snowy petals softly pave
The ground, and thread the rainy breeze,
I share your songs, through charmed hours,
With my sworn friends, the leaves and flowers.

To a blackbird singing in London

Sing on, dear bird! Bring the old rapturous pain,
In this great town, where I no welcome find.
Show me the murmuring forest in your mind,
And April's fragile cups, brimful of rain.
O sing me far away, that I may hear
The voice of grass, and, weeping, may be blind
To slights and lies and friends that prove unkind.
Sing till my soul dissolves into a tear,
Glimmering within a chaliced daffodil.
So, when the stately sun with burning breath
Absorbs my being, I'll dream that he is Death,
Great Death, the undisdainful. By his will
No more unlovely, haunting all things fair,
I'll seek some kinder life in the golden air.

The little sorrow

Within my heart a little sorrow crept
And wept, and wept.
Below the lilt of happiest melodies
I heard his sighs,
And cried—'You little alien in my heart,
Depart! Depart!'

Amid the loud, discordant sounds of fate,
I listening wait—
Not hoping that a song can reach my ear:
But just to hear
That little weeping grief I once bade cease
Would now be peace.

Treasures (for G.E.M.)

These are my treasures: just a word, a look,
A chiming sentence from his favourite book,
A large, blue, scented blossom that he found
And plucked for me in some enchanted ground,
A joy he planned for us, a verse he made
Upon a birthday, the increasing shade
Of trees he planted by the waterside,
The echo of a laugh, his tender pride
In those he loved, his hand upon my hair,
The dear voice lifted in his evening prayer.

How safe they must be kept! So dear, so few,
And all I have to last my whole life through.
A silver mesh of loving words entwining,
At every crossing thread a tear-drop shining,
Shall close them in. Yet since my tears may break
The slender thread of brittle words, I'll make
A safer, humbler hiding-place apart,
And lock them in the fastness of my heart.

The difference

I walk among the daisies, as of old;
But he comes never more by lane or fold.
The same warm speedwell-field is dark with dew;
But he's away beyond a deeper blue.
A year to-day we saw the same flowers grow —
Last May! Last May! A century ago.

Above the speedwell leans the rosy tree
From which he plucked an apple bough for me.
Not all the blossom on the branches left
Can fill the place of that sweet bough bereft;
And none can fill the heart that loved him so
Last May! Last May! Eternities ago.

Winter sunrise

All colours from the frozen earth have died,
And only shadow stains the cold, white snow:
But in the air the April tints abide;
Intangibly and radiantly they grow.
There bloom immortal crocuses, beside
A live-rose hedge, and irises that grow
Along a far green inlet—circling wide
Anemone fields where none but stars may go.
The ardours of a thousand springs are there;
Through infinite deeps they quicken, bright and tender:
In that sequestered garden of the air
No icy pall is heavy on the splendour.
Since you are not in the wintry world to love me,
How softly painted flushes Death above me!

Hunger

Not for the dear things said do I weep now;
Not for your deeds of quiet love and duty
Does my heart freeze and starve since you endow
Cold death with beauty.

Just for the look of utter comprehension;
The dear gay laugh that only true hearts know;
For these I would from life's severe detention
Arise and go.

The lad out there

Oh, Powers of Love, if still you lean
Above a world so black with hate,
Where yet—as it has ever been—
The loving heart is desolate,
Look down upon the lad I love,
(My brave lad, tramping through the mire)—
I cannot light his welcoming fire,
Light Thou the stars for him above!
Now nights are dark and mornings dim,
Let him in his long watching know
That I too count the minutes slow
And light the lamp of love for him.
The sight of death, the sleep forlorn,
The old homesickness vast and dumb—
Amid these things, so bravely borne,
Let my long thoughts about him come.
I see him in the weary file;
So young he is, so dear to me,
With ever-ready sympathy
And wistful eyes and cheerful smile.
However far he travels on,
Thought follows, like the willow-wren
That flies the stormy seas again
To lands where her delight is gone.
Whatever he may be or do
While absent far beyond my call,
Bring him, the long day's march being through,
Safe home to me some evenfall!

To mother, Christmas, 1920

Within the doorway of your room to-night
I stood, and saw your little treasures all
Set out beneath the golden candle-light,
While silver chimes haunted the evenfall.
Here was the robin, very round and bright,
Painted by one of us with fingers small,
And childish presents, bought with grave delight,
For many an ancient Christmas festival.
And while I looked, dear mother, I thought of those
Great dreams that men have dreamed—music like flame,
The lovely works of many a deathless name,
Poetry blooming like a fragrant rose;
And knew God kept them in His house above,
As you our gifts, from the greatness of His love.

Alone

The lonely cuckoo calls
With a long hollow sound among the rocks
Of sun-touched sandstone, and the echo falls
Between the straight red pines to me, and knocks
Upon my heart again and yet again.
It thrills me
With some mysterious mingled joy and pain
That slumbers in the echoing refrain
And stills me.

If only you were here,
We'd go together through the buckler-fern
And watch the nuthatch climbing to his dear;
Then—so that you might follow—I would turn,
And, smiling, mount the steep, and leaning so
Above you,
Await your laughing kiss with eyes a-glow.
Ah! foolish dream—you do not even know
I love you.

Eros

Before his coming thunder breaks;
In plunging fires his way he takes;
Beneath his feet the daisies die,
And night looms darkly in his eye.
So let him come!
Let every silver, trilling bird be dumb!
Let the white daisies drooping lie
Crushed by his pitiless urgency.

He gives no soft or honied kiss,
Nor sings melodious rhapsodies
Of easy joy and bright reward:
His beauty is a flaming sword.
So let him come!
Let every, silver, trilling bird be dumb!
Let the white daisies drooping lie
Crushed by his pitiless urgency.

When the thorn blows

Dawn glimmers white beyond the burning hill
Where sunbeams light a fire in every tree.
The morning bird is singing clear and shrill;
And oh, my love! when will you come to me?

The daisies whitely sleep beneath the dew;
On the wet road the stones are fair to see;
Cloudy, the blackthorn floats upon the blue;
And oh, my love! when will you come to me?

The wind came walking in the shaken wood;
He shouted from the mountains and the sea.
By the pale thorn he paused, in lover's mood —
And oh, my love! when will you come to me?.

My heart has blossomed meekly as the thorn;
It has its dews, and daisies two or three.
The heavens quicken, green as April corn —
And oh, my love! when will you come to me?

'How short a while'

How short a while—eternities gone by—
It is since book and candle, half the night,
Consumed the hours, and in the first grey light
I turned and strove for slumber wearily:
But the sad past complained too mournfully,
And wept before me till the dawn grew white;
And the stark future, stripped of all delight,
Loomed up so near—I could but wake and sigh.

Now they are gone. I lie with ungirt will
And unlit candle, sleeping quietly.
Love flows around me with its calm and blessing;
I can but let it take me, and be still,
And know that you, beloved, though far from me,
All night are with me—comforting, caressing.

'Be still, you little leaves'

Be still, you little leaves! nor tell your sorrow
To any passing bat or hovering owl
Or the low-splashing, restless water-fowl.
You flowering rushes, sigh not till to-morrow;
Come not, sad wind, out of your caverns eerie:
My love is sleeping, and my love is weary.

'Ah, do not be so sweet!'

Ah, do not be so sweet!
For if you only go across the street
The moment is a year.
I hate the careless feet that hurry on
And know not you are near.
An instant fled—and life so swiftly gone,
And you so very dear.

Ah, do not be so kind!
There is so much of beauty in your mind.
When low your dark head lies
In sleep, I see your brow and mouth possessed
With some old agonies,
And thirst for morning—broken, sad, distressed
Until I see your eyes.

Ah, do not be so dear!
The heavy-handed world, if it should hear
And watch us jealously,
Would steal upon our love's secure retreat
And rob our treasury.
Let us be wise, then; do not be too sweet,
Too dear, too kind to me!

Autumn

When autumn winds are on the hill
And darkly rides the wasting moon,
I creep within your arms, and still
Am safe in the golden heart of June.

November

When on my merry garden cold fogs rise
And from these golden trees the blossoms fall;
When in the hollow, painted morning skies
No more the sweet birds call;
When music dies, and colour blurs to grey,
And laughter slips into a sob and fails;
When all my troops of dreams, serene and gay,
Are frozen nightingales—
Where shall I turn, since God is far withdrawn,
And heaven a palace fallen in the sea?
How can I live, a stranger to the dawn?
Ah, who will comfort me?
You, dear, with sadness of unflinching sight,
Behold the pitiful world, the pitiless sky,
Strong in the midst of storm and cold and night,
More great, more brave, than I;
And I could live with sorrow all my days,
Having your word of praise.

Humble folk

Above our lane two rows of larches lean,
And lissom, rosy pines with wild black hair—
One slim, bright-fingered chestnut in between.
In blossom-time and berry-time and snow
Are muffled sounds of feet that come and go
For ever, from the cones and falling spines
And the sad, homeless rhythm of the pines.
These are our friends; we feel the griefs they bear;
We know the larches' thin young April song;
The heavy, dark endeavour of the cone
That goes alone
Among the thick, obliterating dust—
Impelled by something faint and strong
Within her, by the lust
Of death, towards the red and living tree.
Our fingers and the chestnut's touch and hold
The blue light and the gold,
And in a little drop them listlessly.
We know so few things more than these—
The larch that moans in rain
And every March puts roses on again;
The wise, mute chestnut listening to the bees;
The pine
That drinks the icy wind like wine.
We ask no better birth than their brown roots;
We dare not dream of immortality
Unshared by their brown fruits.
And when the wild bee's voice
Grows faint for us, we only ask to lie
Like two straight trees cut down together,
Not fearing any weather,
Too soundly sleeping even to rejoice.

Winter

If I should be the first to go away
Out of the golden sunlight of our peace,
When the dear sacrament of common day
And lowly, love-empurpled tasks shall cease;
When the old books beside the evening fire
Neglected lie, and closed the garden gate,
And from our hill the blossom-tinted shire
Gathers for us an air disconsolate—
Then, oh beloved! hold me close, so close,
Nearer than thought of pain or sad regret;
So wrapped in you, I even should forget
The lifelong dread of parting; and the rose
Of June would flower for me, though cold and slow
And weary on our roof-tree fell the snow.
Speak to me then with that most tender voice,
Wherein I hear the forest murmur fall,
The songs of the corn and velvet-throated doves
That each on each with muted music call,
Minding each other of their leafy loves.
So gathered safe within your voice, your eyes,
Your dear protecting smile, I shall not know
When the black frost sets in, the dark wind cries.
For as the squirrel and the mole, so warm
Within their snow-proof chambers, and the bee
Walled in with summer, wake not, though the storm
Besieges hive and forest—so with me
All will be well; for, sealed in dreamless slumbers,
I shall not know my world is desolate.
Ages may pass, like leaves that no man numbers,
While in the nest of love I hibernate.

The thought

As a pale moth passes
In the April grasses,
So I come and go,
Softlier than snow.
Swifter than a star
Through the heart I flee,
Singing things that are
And things that cannot be.
I whisper to the mole
And the cold fish in the sea,
And to man's wistful soul
God sendeth me.
As a grey moth passes
In October grasses,
So I come and go,
Softlier than snow.

Little things

Among the purple buds, like laden censers,
Careless upon the wind the catkins swing;
They lay a golden spell upon the morning.
From their soft glee how many trees will spring?

The tiny spiders on wych elms in May,
Of rare pale green; the young and downy bee,
Singing her first low song; the white ant's cradle—
They crowd upon us with their mystery.

The fourfold creamy blackthorn buds are folded
Close on green marvels, as upon a treasure
A child's hand; the five pearl doors open softly—
There's a gold house where some elf takes his pleasure.

On the small pear-bud, with its silver calyx,
Some one (I know not who) has set a cross,
Rosy and glowing. On that Calvary-rood
Love might hang long, and know not pain or loss.

Fire-white from curtains of intensest blue
The centre of the speedwell gleams; so fair,
So mystic-frail the tremulous pollen-worlds,
Divinity itself seems slumbering there.

The shell

What has the sea swept up?
A Viking oar, long mouldered in the peace
Of grey oblivion? Some dim-burning bowl
Of unmixed gold, from far-off island feasts?
Ropes of old pearls? Masses of ambergris?
Something of elfdom from the ghastly isles
Where white-hot rocks pierce through the flying spindrift?
Or a pale sea-queen, close wound in a net of spells?

Nothing of these. Nothing of antique splendours
That have a weariness about their names:
But—fresh and new, in frail transparency,
Pink as a baby's nail, silky and veined
As a flower petal—this casket of the sea,
One shell.

A hawthorn berry

How sweet a thought,
How strange a deed,
To house such glory in a seed—
A berry, shining rufously,
Like scarlet coral in the sea!
A berry, rounder than a ring,
So round, it harbours everything;
So red, that all the blood of men
Could never paint it so again.
And, as I hold it in my hand,
A fragrance steals across the land:
Rich, on the wintry heaven, I see
A white, immortal hawthorn-tree.

The snowdrop

Three softly curved white sepals veined with light,
Three green-lined petals, guarding frugal gold,
And all so strong to fold or to unfold!
Snow thunders from the bending pines. How slight
This frail, sheathed stem! Yet all unbent it springs,
So swift in stoopings and recoverings.

In the pale sunshine, with frail wings unfurled,
Comes to the bending snowdrop the first bee.
She gives her winter honey prudently;
And faint with travel in a bitter world,
The bee makes music, tentative and low,
And spring awakes and laughs across the snow.

The vision

In the busy tongues of spring
There's an angel carolling.
Kneeling low in any place,
We may see the Father's face;
Standing quiet anywhere,
Hear our Lady speaking fair;
And in daily marketings
Feel the rush of beating wings.
Watching always, wonderingly,
All the faces passing by,
There we see through pain and wrong
Christ look out, serene and strong.

The vagrant

Who came so close then?—
Brushed the wet lilac into mellow laughter;
Set the smooth blackbird at his golden weaving
Making no stir at all, no footprint leaving;
Travelling westward, all things following after?

Who whispered secrets?—
Tempted the worm up from her winter hiding
To lie her length in the rain of early summer?
Who cut the leaf-buds open? What new-comer
Told the tall heron the place of her abiding?

Some one has been here:
Not the rough, drunken wind who shouts and wanders,
Trampling the woodpath; neither dawn nor gloaming
Nor the young airs in cowslip-garlands roaming.
Who was it then? The muted spirit ponders.

Close by the water
Wrapt in a dream, I saw a faint reflection
Like a wayfarer, calm and worn of features,
Clad in the brown of leaves and little creatures,
Stern as the moorland, russet of complexion.

Dark in the shadow
Fathomless eyes met mine with thought unspoken,
Wistful, yet deep within them laughter lingered.
With sunburnt hands a wooden flute he fingered
Under the thorn-tree, where the lights are broken.

Then the green river
Dimmed like a misted mirror; blossom only
Whitened it, on the covert water lying.
Westward along the willows ran a sighing.
Herd-like the clouds went home and left me lonely.

Over the meadows
Wild music came like spray upon the shingle;
Piping the world to mating; changing, calling
Low to the heart like doves when rain is falling.
Surely he cut his flute in Calvary's dingle?

I rose and followed.
Right to the sunset-bars, yet never found him.
Backward along the edge of night returning
Sadly, I watched the slip of moon upburning
Silver, as if she drank the life around him.

In the dark aspens
Hark! a flute note; so still he's at his playing.
Tawny the furrows lie—his homely vesture.
Labourers pass: I see his very gesture—
Vigorous, tranquil, with his music straying.

Now I know surely
Who set the birds a-fire and touched the grasses—
Silent, without a footprint, no shade throwing.
Infinite worlds his shadow: all things growing
Stir with his breathing, follow as he passes.

The wild rose

Five pointed sepals with a pearly sheen
Uphold the frail cup's curved transparency,
White-veined below, and flushing tenderly
Towards the brim. A shadow lies between
Each loose-curved petal, and the scent—so keen,
So sweet—is very wine of joy to me.
The humming honey-people eagerly
Enjoy this loving-cup among the green.
We share together, the butterfly, the bee
And I, and the little beetles that gleam and shine.
And yet one more, my spirit whisperingly
Has spoken of, whose banquet is divine.
Deep down within the chalice I can see
The gold He left there as His kingly fee.

Thresholds

So here is come the night of nights!
On every pine a star is kindled.
Too slowly cumbrous summer dwindled;
But now the frostly silence hums
And comfort in the boundless darkness comes
Along the heights.

Through weary times of brooding harm
We waited. Now the hour is ringing.
In haste we leave the wicket swinging
And whisper, splashing through the mire,
Of music and of colours bright like fire
At Thresholds Farm.

Up yonder on the hill-side stark
The long sheds crouch beneath the larches.
We smile to think the whole world marches
With us to where the shippen gleams
And flower-pale faces cluster, keen as dreams,
Against the dark.

We hear the cow-chains lift and fall;
We almost feel the ageless splendour
Of Child and Mother, warm and tender;
We run and softly push the door. . .
The mice go shrieking down the lonely floor,
The empty stall.

The door

I heard humanity, through all the years,
Wailing, and beating on a dark, vast door
With urgent hands and eyes blinded by tears.
Will none come forth to them for evermore?
Like children at their father's door, who wait,
Crying 'Let us in!' on some bright birthday morn,
Quite sure of joy, they grow disconsolate,
Left in the cold unanswered and forlorn.
Forgetting even their toys in their alarms,
They only long to climb on father's bed
And cry their terrors out in father's arms.
And maybe, all the while, their father's dead.

The land within

This is a land of forests, and of meres
Stirless and deep, replenished with my tears.
Here the pine harps, and many voices moan
Within the cedar, crying, 'Lone! Alone!'
Sharp on green heaven the green ice peaks arise
Through the deep snows of thawless purities.
Ten thousand stars are drowned within the lake,
Beneath grey ice. And while the branches break,
The million crystals shining there arow
Can never fall, though every tempest blow.
Only the rush, with brown and broken spear,
Tells of the host of summer mustering here,
Where now the reeds, encrusted stiff with glass,
Sound a faint music, faintly sigh 'Alas!'
Where are the birds that with blue flash would make
Traffic between blue sky and bluer lake,
Ripping the water with a long, keen wing,
Then setting rosy breasts arow to sing?
O, they are fled, my soul! Fled far away
To some gold tree in Spain or Africa.

Was there a sound of leaves here once, and streams
Gurgling on pebbles? (In dreams, my soul! in dreams.)
Galleons of golden lilies then could ride
Safely, though coot and moorhen stirred the tide,
Swimming with all their young; and loud sweet cries
Fell from the mountains where the curlew haunted
Green mossy cwms, sun-drenched and thrice enchanted;
And somewhere in the lake's confused reflections,
Remote and fair as childhood's recollections,
Smothered in wavering lilac leaves, and blurred
With bloom, the shadow of a gable stirred
With every tide, and a twisted chimney flowered
In pale blue smoke, that in the water towered
Downward. And through those deeps, pillared and aisled

Came a brown woodman, and a boy who smiled,
Running towards the shifting wicket-gate,
And waved an under-water hand, to spy
One leaning from the casement—that was I.

Where was that cottage with its lilac trees,
Its windows wide, its garden drowsed with bees?
Where stood the echoing glade whence the faggot came
To turn the evening hours to one warm flame?
And that brown woodman, where and whence was he—
That woodman, with the eyes that dazzled me
Far more than rosy fire or golden gleams
Of April? O, in dreams, my soul! in dreams.

The ancient gods

Certainly there were splashings in the water,
Certainly there were shadows on the hill,
Dark with the leaves of purple-spotted orchis;
But now all's still.

It may be that the catkin-covered sallow,
With her illusive, glimmering surprise,
Pale golden-tinted as a tall young goddess,
Deceived my eyes;

And the white birches wading in the margin,
Each one a naked and a radiant god,
Dazzled me; and the foam was flung by currents
Where no feet trod.

Only I know I saw them—stately, comely,
Within the leafy shadows of the stream;
They woke amid the shallow, singing water
A fading gleam.

They left no trail for any beast to follow,
No track upon the moss for man to trace;
In a long, silent file up-stream they vanished
With measured pace.

The hollow water curved about their ankles
Like amber; splashes glistened on their thighs;
Sun barred their lifted heads and their far-seeing
Yet sightless eyes.

Some were like women, with deep hair of willows,
Bare breasts and gracious arms and long, smooth hips,
And the red roses of desire half frozen
Upon their lips:

But most were massive-browed and massive-shouldered
And taller than the common height of men.
They went as those that have not home nor kindred,
Nor come again.

Still, where the birches fingered their reflection,
The thrushes chanted to the evening sky;
Still the grey wagtails raced across the shingle
As they went by.

Beyond the furthest of the saffron shallows
I lost them in the larches' rainy green,
And only saw the stretches of marsh-mallows
Where they had been.

You say the sallow and the birch deceived me:
But I know well that I beheld to-day
The ancient gods, unheralded, majestic,
Upon their way.

Colomen

The doves that coo in Colomen
Are never heard by mortal men,
But when a human creature passes
Underneath the churchyard grasses,
In deep voices, velvet-warm,
They tell of ancient perils, storm
Long hushed, and hopes withered and dead,
And joys a long while harvested.

There was a lady small and thin
(Oh, grave! Why did you let her in?)
Her voice was sad as a dove's, her feet
Went softly through the yellow wheat,
Like stars that haunt the evening west.
Hers was the tall, round, sunny cote
Whence, as she called, her doves would float
Softly, on arm and shoulder rest,
Until the lady, leaning so,
Under the feathers of rose and snow,
Wing of azure and purple plume,
Was like a slim tree bent with bloom.

And still, at Colomen, they say,
When midsummer has stolen away
The last arch primrose, and swiftly fall
Hawthorn petals, wan as a pall,
And the grave blackbirds, that of late
Shouted the sun up, meditate,
You hear about the ruined cote
A mighty, muted sound of wings,
And faint, ghostly flutterings.
Then, if your death is near, you see
A lady standing like a tree
Bent down with blossom. Long ago
Her little joy, her long woe!

In an April dawn of rose and flame
A poor, travelling painter came
Through tasselled woods, and in the tower
Beheld the lady, like a flower —
A pale flower beneath the hill,
Trembling when the air is still,
Broken when the storms are wild,
The lady looked on him, and smiled.
Woe, woe to Colomen,
Where never lovers come again,
Laughing in the morning air!

Dew decked the lady's hair
Because the lilac, purple and tall,
Saw her beauty and let fall
All her silver, all her sweet.
In dove-grey dawns their lips
In the room beneath the tower
Where the drowsy sunlight smote
Seldom, and the air would creep
Stealthily and half asleep,
While stillness held the dancing mote,
And croonings fell from the ivied cote
With a musical, low roar,
Like summer seas on a fairy shore.

The boding wind had moaned of loss;
The boding shadow laid a cross
From the barred window to their feet;
The doves made a heart-broken, sweet
Clamour of some eerie thing.
They did not hear nor understand
How soon love is withered away
Like a flower on a frosty day!

Early in a summer dawn
When the shadows of the doves were drawn
Down the roof and from the clover

The bees' low roar came up, her lover
Finished her portrait, thin and small
And pale, with an ethereal
Sweet air, because he had seen her soul
Come to the threshold when she stole
To meet him. There for ever she stood
Like a silver fairy in a wood
Or a may-tree in the moonlight.
He told her of his dream's delight,
How they would dwell alone, aloof,
With doves crooning on the roof.

He had painted through a sapphire June
Into a thunderous dark July.
Alas! How fleet is spring! How soon
From all their little windows fly
The doves of joy! In an evil hour
Her sister saw him leave the tower.

For all her simple country grace,
Hers was a haughty, lordly race.
When night was thick and black above,
They sent the press-gang for her love.

All day, beside the memoried cote
She lay so still they thought her dead,
Her doves, that wheeled above her head.
But in her eyes a wild, remote,
Inhuman sorrow slumbered.

When next the clover called the bee,
Where was she? Ah, where was she?

She dragged her leaden limbs across
The grey lawns, to hear the sound
That turned a sword within her wound
And made her agony of loss
So keen that if she held her breath

She almost heard the feet of death.
When all her thronging pigeons cooed
Around, with outspread arms she stood.
She seemed a pale and slender tree,
But with snow and not with bloom—
Bent lower towards the tomb.

She would be free of the distress
That men call joy, the littleness
That men call life—as birds are free.
So in the dewy morning hour
She hanged herself within the tower,
Beside her portrait, spirit-fair,
With these words written: 'We come again,
And ours the house of Colomen.'

Her cousins came and found her there,
While high against the painted dawn
Her pigeons—rosy, white and fawn,
Coal-black and mottled—wheeled in the air.
But while they gazed, weeping aloud,
Around the tower a silence fell.
The doves wheeled high: they could not tell
Which were birds and which was cloud.

A haunted silence held the tower,
Wherein the portrait's living eyes
Watched the dead lady with surprise,
Like a flower that gazes on a flower.
No doves returned there evermore.
The spiders wove about the door
Intricate tapestries of time,
That held the dew and held the rime.
And from the house of Colomen,
Like water from a frozen strand,
Failed the voices of maids and men,
Shrivelled the heart, shrivelled the hand,
Till there within the arching wood

No face was left but the painted face,
No sound was left of the human race,
But only the sound of doves that cooed
Sadly, intermittently —
Wheeling doves that none can see
But dying men who wander here
And see a picture, glassy-clear,
Where the milky hawthorn-blossom falls
And from the elm a blackbird calls:
Then softly from the ruined cote
A pigeon coos — and faint, remote,
A hundred pigeons answer low,
Voicing the lady's ancient woe;
And then they see her, very fair
And fragile in the scented air;
On arms and shoulders doves alight,
Multiple-tinted, like a bright
Tapestry that time has faded.
Softly purple, lilac-shaded,
The lady standeth, like a tree
Bent down with blossom....

With thanks to the Literary Heritage - West Midlands
http://www.literaryheritage.org.uk

Lightning Source UK Ltd.
Milton Keynes UK
12 July 2010

156900UK00002B/190/P